BABY PIP EATS

······················

AMIE HARPER

MURDOCH BOOKS
SYDNEY · LONDON

ALL ABOUT AMIE

Amie Harper has always been passionate about preparing and sharing delicious, nutritious meals among family and friends. With the exciting arrival of her first child, she turned her attention to smaller servings and a simplified palate to please baby Pip.
She hopes to inspire you to plate up a creative variety of meals for your baby and family, so that they may grow up healthy, happy and one day to be as excited about food as their mummies and daddies are! With a degree in food science and nutrition, Amie has over ten years' experience as a food technologist for some of the world's largest consumer goods companies. She has also worked as a freelance food stylist and recipe writer for magazines such as *The Australian Women's Weekly*, *Gourmet Traveller* and *Good Taste*.

amieeats.com.au

FOR
BABY PIP

· · · · · · · · · · · · · ·

THANK YOU TO
ELLE-ROSE MURRELL
FOR ALL YOUR HELP

IS FOR AVOCADO

· ·

AVOCADO PURÉE

EAT ME FROM: 6 MONTHS
SOURCE OF: MONO & POLYUNSATURATED
FATS, VITAMIN A, D & E
SERVES: 1 BABY & 1 ADULT

Mash 1 peeled and seeded avocado with the juice of ½ lemon.
Serve on fresh bread or toast and with a boiled free-range egg
and chicken soup (see page 8) for a complete nutritious meal.

IS FOR BROCCOLI

· ·

BROCCOLI AU GRATIN

EAT ME FROM: 7–8 MONTHS (ONCE CHEWING DEVELOPED)
SOURCE OF: VITAMIN A & C, CALCIUM & IRON
SERVES: 1 BABY & FAMILY OF 4

Preheat the oven to 190°C (375°F). To make the white sauce,
melt 2 tbsp butter in a non-stick saucepan over medium heat, then
add 2 tbsp plain (all-purpose) flour and cook, whisking, for 1 minute until
a roux forms. Gradually pour in 625 ml (21½ fl oz/2½ cups) milk and whisk
vigorously until all the lumps have disappeared and the sauce has thickened.
Season with sea salt and cracked black pepper to taste and set aside.
Chop 1 head each of cauliflower and broccoli into florets. Peel and dice
1 small sweet potato. Steam the vegetables for 5 minutes or until soft when
pierced with a fork. Place into a large baking dish and pour the white sauce
over to cover. Sprinkle with 50 g (1¾ oz/½ cup) grated cheese. Bake for
30–35 minutes or until golden brown. Serve and enjoy immediately.

IS FOR CHICKEN

CHICKEN SOUP

EAT ME FROM: 7–8 MONTHS (ONCE CHEWING DEVELOPED)
SOURCE OF: IRON & ZINC
SERVES: 1 BABY & FAMILY OF 4

Heat a non-stick sauté pan over medium heat and add 1 tbsp olive oil or butter. Add 1 washed and chopped leek (pale part only) and cook, stirring occasionally, for 5 minutes until soft. Add 2 diced carrots, 2 diced celery sticks and 2 tsp chopped thyme. Cook for a further 3 minutes. Add 1 kg (2 lb 4 oz) chopped chicken thigh fillets and cook, stirring, for 5 minutes. Add 1.5 litres (52 fl oz/6 cups) water or chicken stock (homemade stock is best as it's less salty, or use a reduced-salt one) and bring to a boil, then reduce the heat to a gentle simmer and cook for 1–1½ hours. Alternatively you can transfer the mixture to a slow cooker after the stock has been added and cook for 4 hours on the fast setting or 6–8 hours on the slow setting. Remove the chicken from the soup and shred into small pieces. Return the chicken to the soup, stir through, then serve with bread and mashed pumpkin for dipping.

Try: You can use diced skinless chicken breast fillets instead of thighs; they don't take as long to cook, so reduce the simmering time to 30 minutes (or until the chicken is cooked through and the veggies are soft). I don't recommend using breast meat if you're cooking this in a slow cooker, though, as the meat tends to dry out.

IS FOR DAL

DAL

EAT ME FROM: 6 MONTHS
SOURCE OF: IRON, DIETARY FIBRE,
PROTEIN, B GROUP VITAMINS & ZINC
SERVES: 1 BABY & FAMILY OF 4

Place 410 g (14½ oz/2 cups) washed red lentils, 2 peeled and diced carrots,
½ peeled and diced sweet potato, 80 g (2¾ oz/½ cup) chopped pumpkin (squash),
1 peeled and chopped potato, 1.5 litres (52 fl oz/6 cups) water or chicken
stock and ½ bunch finely chopped coriander (cilantro) in a large saucepan.
Bring to a boil over low heat and simmer for 15 minutes. If you'd like a looser
consistency for baby, stir through some more water to heat through,
then serve with baked potatoes, pasta or naan bread, with natural yoghurt,
more chopped fresh coriander and fresh lime or lemon alongside.

Health hint: Add a squeeze of lemon juice to your dal. The vitamin C
in a fresh lemon helps improve iron absorption, especially of non-haem iron
(found in plant-based foods like lentils). Spices can be added depending
on your baby's tastes; I like to add 2 tsp ground cumin, 2 tsp ground
coriander and 1 tsp smoked paprika at the beginning of cooking.

IS FOR EGG

EGG FRENCH TOAST

EAT ME FROM: 7–8 MONTHS (ONCE CHEWING DEVELOPED)
SOURCE OF: PROTEIN, VITAMIN A & D
SERVES: 1 BABY & 2 ADULTS

In a bowl, lightly beat 2 free-range eggs with 1 tbsp milk and a pinch
of salt and pepper (optional). Working one slice at a time, dip 4 slices of bread
into the egg mixture, turning once. Heat a non-stick frying pan over medium
heat and add 2 tsp olive oil. Fry the bread, turning once, until golden brown.
Serve and enjoy immediately.

Try: Add 1 tbsp chopped fresh mixed herbs (such as dill, chives or parsley)
to the egg mixture before dipping the bread, and sprinkle with more
herbs and grated cheese just before serving. Use a cookie cutter to cut
the bread into cute shapes your baby will love.

IS FOR FRITTERS

FRITTERS WITH SWEET POTATO & RICOTTA

EAT ME FROM: 7–8 MONTHS (ONCE CHEWING DEVELOPED)
SOURCE OF: VITAMIN A & C
SERVES: 1 BABY & 2 ADULTS

Peel and grate 1 sweet potato and 1 potato. Combine in a bowl with 2 free-range eggs, 185 g (6½ oz/¾ cup) ricotta cheese and 75 g (2½ oz/½ cup) plain (all-purpose) flour. Heat a non-stick frying pan over medium heat and add 1 tbsp of butter or vegetable oil. Working in batches, add heaped tablespoonfuls of the mixture to the pan and press down to flatten slightly. Cook, turning once, for 5 minutes. Repeat with the remaining mixture, adding more butter or oil as needed; you'll get about 12 fritters in all. Season and serve with avocado purée, natural yoghurt, relish and a wedge of lemon.

Dairy-free: Omit the ricotta cheese and add an extra egg to the mixture instead. Cook the fritters in oil. Garnish with fresh chopped herbs in place of natural yoghurt.

IS FOR 'GOOGY' EGG

· ·

'GOOGY' EGG TOAST

EAT ME FROM: 7–8 MONTHS (ONCE CHEWING DEVELOPED)
SOURCE OF: PROTEIN, VITAMIN A & D
SERVES: 1 BABY AND 2 ADULTS

Cut out the centres of 4 slices of bread using a cookie cutter or a glass (keep these cut-out pieces to toast and serve). Heat a non-stick frying pan over medium heat and add 2 tsp butter or olive oil. Working in batches depending on the size of your pan, place the bread slices in the pan and carefully crack 1 free-range egg into each hole. Cook, turning once, for 3 minutes or until the eggs are cooked through and the bread is golden. Serve and enjoy immediately.

IS FOR HASH BROWN

HASH BROWNS

EAT ME FROM: 7–8 MONTHS (ONCE CHEWING DEVELOPED)
SOURCE OF: CARBOHYDRATES, POTASSIUM & VITAMIN C
SERVES: 1 BABY & 1 ADULT

Roughly combine 115 g (4 oz/½ cup) cooked mashed potato with
30 g (1 oz/½ cup) cooked broccoli florets and 1 tbsp grated cheese. Heat a
non-stick frying pan over medium heat and add 1 tsp olive oil. Add teaspoonfuls
of the potato mixture to the pan, flattening them slightly. Cook, turning once,
for 3–5 minutes or until lightly golden. Serve immediately.

IS FOR ICE

ICE POPS

EAT ME FROM: 6 MONTHS
SOURCE OF: CALCIUM & VITAMIN C
MAKES: 12 CUBES

Slice the cheeks of 2 mangoes and scoop the flesh from each cheek. Place the mango into a bowl and mash with a fork. Divide the mango evenly among the holes in an ice-cube tray, without filling to the top. Spoon 1 tsp natural yoghurt on top of the mango, then cover and freeze for 2 hours. Remove the ice pops 5 minutes before serving to soften. Serve and enjoy immediately.

IS FOR JAP PUMPKIN

PUMPKIN RISOTTO

EAT ME FROM: 7–8 MONTHS (ONCE CHEWING DEVELOPED)
SOURCE OF: BETA CAROTENE, IRON, VITAMIN C & POTASSIUM
SERVES: 1 BABY & FAMILY OF 4

Heat 1 tbsp olive oil in a non-stick frying pan over medium heat. Add 1 diced brown onion and cook for 3 minutes until soft. Add 2 crushed garlic cloves and cook for 1 minute until fragrant. Add 275 g (9¾ oz/1¼ cups) arborio rice and stir gently for 1 minute. Add 1 litre (35 fl oz/4 cups) chicken stock (homemade is best as it's less salty, or use a reduced-salt one) and 200 g (7 oz) peeled and chopped jap (kent) pumpkin (squash). Cook, stirring regularly, for 20 minutes or until the rice is al dente and the pumpkin is soft. Remove from the heat and stir through 25 g (1 oz/¼ cup) finely grated parmesan. Serve and enjoy immediately.

Try: Substitute butternut squash if jap is unavailable. It has a sweeter flavour (similar to a mix between pumpkin and sweet potato) that your baby will love.

IS FOR KITTY

KITTY CAULIFLOWER PATTIES & AVOCADO BITES

EAT ME FROM: 7–8 MONTHS (ONCE CHEWING DEVELOPED)
SOURCE OF: DIETARY FIBRE & VITAMIN E
SERVES: 1 BABY & FAMILY OF 4

Steam ¼ head of cauliflower, chopped into florets, and 1 diced potato for 8–10 minutes or until very soft. Place the steamed vegetables, 1 tbsp of butter and a dash of milk (optional) in a large bowl and mash with a fork until smooth. Allow to cool, then add 1 free-range egg and 35 g (1¼ oz/¼ cup) plain (all-purpose) flour and stir to combine. Heat a non-stick frying pan over medium heat and add 1 tsp olive oil. Working in batches, drop heaped tablespoonfuls of the mixture into the pan, flattening them slightly. Cook for 5 minutes, turning once, or until golden brown. Season and serve with fresh avocado and lemon slices and enjoy immediately.

Try: Use different sized kitty cookie cutters to make irresistible shapes your baby will love.

IS FOR LEEK

LEEK, POTATO & PARSNIP SOUP

EAT ME FROM: 6 MONTHS
SOURCE OF: VITAMIN K & IRON
SERVES: 1 BABY & FAMILY OF 4

Preheat the oven to 180°C (350°F) and line a large baking tray with baking paper.
Place 8 mini pumpkins (squash) on the prepared tray and bake for 25 minutes or until
softened. Carefully slice off the top of each pumpkin, scoop out the seeds and discard.
Heat 1 tbsp oil in a large saucepan or stockpot over medium heat. Add 1 washed and chopped
leek (pale part only) and cook for 5 minutes, stirring occasionally. Add 4 large diced potatoes,
2 peeled and diced parsnips and 1.25 litres (44 fl oz/5 cups) water or chicken stock and simmer
for 20 minutes or until the vegetables are soft. Remove from the heat and allow the soup to
cool slightly before blending to a smooth purée. Divide evenly among the mini pumpkins,
then serve immediately with natural yoghurt, grated cheese and parsley.

Health hint: Purchased chicken stock can contain a lot of salt, so make your
own if you can or buy a reduced-salt version.

IS FOR MOO COW

MOO COW BURGERS

EAT ME FROM: 7–8 MONTHS (ONCE CHEWING DEVELOPED)
SOURCE OF: IRON, ZINC & PROTEIN
SERVES: 1 BABY & FAMILY OF 4

Combine 500 g (1 lb 2 oz) good-quality minced (ground) beef with
30 g (1 oz/½ cup) fresh breadcrumbs, 1 free-range egg and 1 tbsp chopped
parsley in a bowl. Take teaspoonfuls of the mixture and roll into balls,
then flatten them slightly and set aside.
Heat a non-stick frying pan over medium heat and add 1 tbsp olive oil.
Working in batches, cook the meatballs for 5 minutes, turning once, or until
golden brown and cooked through. Serve immediately with cow-shaped
toast and moo (tomato or barbecue) sauce and enjoy.

IS FOR NOODLES

SOBA NOODLES WITH POACHED CHICKEN, BROCCOLI, FRIED EGG, CHIA SEEDS & TAMARI

EAT ME FROM: 7–8 MONTHS (ONCE CHEWING DEVELOPED)
SOURCE OF: DIETARY FIBRE & ESSENTIAL MINERALS
SERVES: 1 BABY & 2 ADULTS

Cook 1 x 240 g (8½ oz) pack of soba noodles according to the directions, then drain and set aside. Place 2 skinless chicken breast fillets into a saucepan of cool water. Bring to a gentle boil and simmer for 10–12 minutes or until the chicken is cooked through, then remove from the pan and slice into 5 mm (¼ in) thick pieces. Steam ½ head of broccoli, chopped into florets, for 5 minutes until soft, then refresh under cold water. Heat a large non-stick frying pan over medium heat and add 2 tsps olive oil. Crack 3 free-range eggs into the pan and cook for 2–3 minutes or until cooked through, then remove and set aside. Divide the cooked noodles, the broccoli and poached chicken among bowls, sprinkle with a small handful of chia seeds and top with tamari to taste. Serve with a fried egg and enjoy immediately.

Vegetarian option: Use tofu instead of chicken.

IS FOR OWL

OWL VEGETABLES

EAT ME FROM: 7–8 MONTHS (ONCE CHEWING DEVELOPED)
SOURCE OF: VITAMIN A, CALCIUM & PROTEIN
SERVES: 1 BABY & FAMILY OF 4

Slice 500 g (1 lb 2 oz) peeled butternut pumpkin (squash) lengthways into 2 cm (¾ in) thick flat slices. Cut out shapes using an owl or other animal-shaped cookie cutter, repeating until all the pumpkin has been used. Steam the pumpkin owls for 8 minutes or until tender. Cook 400 g (14 oz) orecchiette pasta according to the packet directions, then drain, reserving 2–3 tbsps of the cooking liquid. Combine the cooked pasta, pumpkin owls, 230 g (8 oz/1 cup) ricotta cheese and enough cooking liquid to get the texture you desire. Season to taste, then stir through a small handful of chopped herbs. Serve and enjoy immediately.

IS FOR PASTA

PASTA WITH PUMPKIN, PEAS & BACON

EAT ME FROM: 7–8 MONTHS (ONCE CHEWING DEVELOPED)
SOURCE OF: VITAMIN A, CARBOHYDRATES
SERVES: 1 BABY & FAMILY OF 4

Steam 400 g (14 oz) peeled and chopped pumpkin (squash) for 8 minutes or until tender, then set aside. Heat a frying pan over medium heat and add 1 tsp olive oil. Cook 1 diced onion and 2 finely chopped garlic cloves for 3 minutes until fragrant. Add 4 diced rindless rashers of bacon and cook for a further 2 minutes, then remove from the heat and set aside. Meanwhile, cook 400 g (14 oz) fettuccine according to the packet directions, then drain, reserving 2–3 tbsps of the cooking liquid. Cook 200 g (7 oz) frozen peas according to the packet directions. Combine the steamed pumpkin, hot pasta, 100 g (3½ oz) crumbled goat's feta and the reserved cooking liquid in a large bowl and mash together lightly, then stir through the peas and the bacon mixture. Divide among bowls, serve and enjoy immediately.

IS FOR QUICHE

ROASTED SWEET POTATO, GOAT'S FETA, PARMESAN & PARSLEY QUICHE

EAT ME FROM: 7–8 MONTHS (ONCE CHEWING DEVELOPED)
SOURCE OF: VITAMIN A & K
MAKES: 1 X 20 CM (8 IN) ROUND QUICHE,
TO SERVE 1 BABY & FAMILY OF 4

Preheat the oven to 175°C (330°F) and line a baking tray with baking paper.
Peel and dice 1 large sweet potato. Place on the prepared tray and roast for 35 minutes
until tender, then set aside. Whisk together 5 free-range eggs and 60 ml (2 fl oz/¼ cup)
thin (pouring) cream and set aside. Line a 20 cm (8 in) round cake tin with baking paper
and sprinkle the base with 1 tbsp grated parmesan and 2 tsps chopped parsley.
Arrange the cooked sweet potato and 100 g (3½ oz) crumbled goat's feta evenly over
the base, then pour in the egg mixture to cover. Sprinkle over an extra 1 tbsp grated
parmesan and 2 tsps chopped parsley and bake for 30–35 minutes or until set
and slightly golden brown. Serve and enjoy immediately.

Health hint: Thickened cream contains additives, so use regular cream for this.

IS FOR RAGU

BEEF & MUSHROOM RAGU WITH PASTA

EAT ME FROM: 7–8 MONTHS (ONCE CHEWING DEVELOPED)
SOURCE OF: IRON, ZINC & PROTEIN
SERVES: 1 BABY & FAMILY OF 4

Heat a non-stick sauté pan over medium heat and add 1 tbsp olive oil. Add 1 diced onion, 2 cloves chopped garlic and 1 tbsp chopped rosemary or thyme and cook, stirring, for 5 minutes. Add 1 tbsp butter and 1 kg (2 lb 4 oz) lightly floured, chopped chuck steak. Cook, stirring occasionally, for 5 minutes until the meat has browned. Add 200 g (7 oz) chopped mushrooms and cook for 3 minutes until the mushrooms have softened. Add 500 ml (17 fl oz/2 cups) water or chicken stock and 600 g (1 lb 5 oz) tomato passata (puréed tomatoes) and bring to a boil. Reduce the heat to a gentle simmer, cover and cook, stirring occasionally, for 3 hours or until the meat has softened and pulls apart easily. Meanwhile, cook 400 g (14 oz) pasta according to the packet directions, then drain and combine with the sauce in a large bowl. Serve with grated parmesan and enjoy immediately.

Try: A slow cooker can be used for this recipe on either the fast or slow setting.

IS FOR SNOWFLAKE

SNOWFLAKE TOASTS WITH SNOW (CAULIFLOWER) SOUP

EAT ME FROM: 7–8 MONTHS (ONCE CHEWING DEVELOPED)
SOURCE OF: VITAMIN A, C & B GROUP VITAMINS & POTASSIUM
SERVES: 1 BABY & FAMILY OF 4

Heat 1 tbsp oil in a large saucepan or stockpot over medium heat. Add 1 washed and chopped leek (pale part only) and cook for 5 minutes, stirring occasionally. Add 1 head of cauliflower chopped into florets, 2 diced potatoes and 1.25 litres (44 fl oz/5 cups) water or chicken stock and simmer for 20 minutes. Remove from the heat and allow to cool slightly before puréeing until smooth. Serve with snowflake cut-out toasts and natural yoghurt.

Health hint: Purchased chicken stock can contain a lot of salt, so make your own if you can or buy a reduced-salt version.

IS FOR TANGERINE

SWEET POTATO & PEAR SOUP

EAT ME FROM: 6 MONTHS
SOURCE OF: DIETARY FIBRE, VITAMIN A & C
SERVES: 1 BABY & FAMILY OF 4

Heat 1 tbsp oil in a large saucepan or stockpot over medium heat. Add 1 diced onion and 1 clove chopped garlic and cook for 3 minutes until soft and fragrant. Add 2 peeled and diced sweet potatoes, 4 peeled and cored pears and 1.25 litres (44 fl oz/5 cups) water or vegetable stock. Bring to a gentle boil and cook for 15–20 minutes until the vegetables are soft. Remove from the heat and allow to cool slightly before puréeing until smooth. Serve and enjoy immediately.

IS FOR UNDER THE SEA

**UNDER THE SEA FRUIT TOAST
WITH BANANA & RICOTTA**

EAT ME FROM: 7-8 MONTHS (ONCE CHEWING DEVELOPED)
SOURCE OF: CALCIUM & DIETARY FIBRE
SERVES: 1 BABY & 2 ADULTS FOR BREAKFAST

Toast 4 slices of fresh fruit bread until golden. Thickly spread fresh ricotta
on the toast and, if you like, use cookie cutters to cut into sea horse
shapes. Cut out a shark shape from a whole peeled banana and place
on top of the toast. Serve and enjoy immediately.

Health hint: I've used fruit and nut bread for the adults here,
but nuts can be an allergen so avoid them for baby.

IS FOR VEGAN

BABY COCONUT NAAN BREAD

EAT ME FROM: 7–8 MONTHS (ONCE CHEWING DEVELOPED)
SOURCE OF: DIETARY FIBRE, IRON & MAGNESIUM
MAKES: 6–8 MINI NAAN BREADS

Combine 300 g (10½ oz/2 cups) plain (all-purpose) spelt flour in a large bowl. Stir through 260 g (9¼ oz/1 cup) coconut yoghurt or 250 ml (9 fl oz/1 cup) coconut cream until just combined. Turn the mixture out onto a lightly floured bench top and knead gently for 1 minute. Take tablespoonfuls of the dough and shape into 6–8 balls, then roll each ball into a 1 cm (½ in) thick round. If you want a garlicky flavour, smash 3 cloves of garlic with 1 tsp sea salt in a mortar and pestle and spread the mixture evenly over the dough rounds. Heat 1 tbsp dairy-free spread (I use Nuttelex) or olive oil in a non-stick frying pan over medium heat. Working in batches, cook the naan, turning once, for 5 minutes or until golden brown and slightly puffed. Serve warm with dal (see page 10).

Try: For a dairy option, use natural yoghurt instead of coconut yoghurt.

IS FOR WOOF

WOOF POTATO PANCAKES

EAT ME FROM: 7–8 MONTHS (ONCE CHEWING DEVELOPED)
SOURCE OF: CARBOHYDRATES, POTASSIUM & VITAMIN C
SERVES: 1 BABY & 2 ADULTS

Combine 345 g (12 oz/1½ cups) cooked mashed potato with 1 free-range egg
and 35 g (1¼ oz/¼ cup) plain (all-purpose) flour. Heat a non-stick frying pan over
medium heat and add 2 tsps olive oil. Add tablespoonfuls of the potato mixture
to the pan, flattening them slightly, and cook, turning once, for 3–5 minutes or until
lightly golden. Repeat until all the mixture has been used up, adding more oil as
needed. Use a doggy-shaped cookie cutter to cut out shapes, then serve with
woof (tomato or barbecue) sauce and enjoy immediately.

IS FOR XOXO KISSES

X'S WITH ORANGE RICOTTA

EAT ME FROM: 7–8 MONTHS (ONCE CHEWING DEVELOPED)
SOURCE OF: DIETARY FIBRE, FOLATE, VITAMIN A & C
MAKES: 12 KISSES

Preheat the oven to 180°C (350°F). Grate or finely chop 3 peeled zucchinis (courgettes), 1 carrot and 1 peeled apple into a large bowl and add 80 g (2¾ oz/½ cup) pitted chopped fresh dates. Add 300 g (10½ oz/2 cups) self-raising flour, 2 free-range eggs and 60 ml (2 fl oz/¼ cup) olive oil and stir to just combine (do not overmix: it's okay if the mixture is a bit lumpy). Lightly grease a 12-hole muffin tray with cooking oil spray. Spoon the mixture evenly among the holes and bake for 20 minutes or until cooked through. Leave to cool for 5 minutes. Combine 230 g (8 oz/1 cup) ricotta cheese with 1 tbsp orange juice. Slice the muffins in half horizontally and spread the ricotta mixture on the bottom half of each muffin. Add chopped strawberries and sandwich the lids on. Serve and enjoy immediately.

IS FOR YELLOW PEACH

YELLOW PEACH CRUNCH

EAT ME FROM: 7–8 MONTHS (ONCE CHEWING DEVELOPED)
SOURCE OF: DIETARY FIBRE, VITAMIN A & C
SERVES: 1 BABY & 2 ADULTS FOR BREAKFAST

Steam 3 halved and de-stoned yellow peaches in a steamer for 5 minutes or until soft. Remove the peaches from the heat and allow to cool slightly. Place a peach half into each bowl, top with natural yoghurt and muesli (granola), then top with another peach half and more yoghurt and muesli. Serve and enjoy immediately.

IS FOR ZUCCHINI

ZUCCHINI WITH SAUTÉED GARLIC & RICOTTA

EAT ME FROM: 7-8 MONTHS (ONCE CHEWING DEVELOPED)
SOURCE OF: GROUP B VITAMINS & DIETARY FIBRE
SERVES: 1 BABY & 2 ADULTS FOR A SNACK

Steam 200 g (7 oz) whole baby zucchinis (courgettes) for 5 minutes or until soft enough for baby. Heat 1 tsp oil in a non-stick frying pan and cook 3 thinly sliced garlic cloves for 2 minutes until fragrant, stirring frequently so the garlic doesn't burn. Sprinkle the garlic and oil over the steamed zucchinis and crumble over some ricotta. Serve and enjoy immediately.

Published in 2016 by Murdoch Books, an imprint of Allen & Unwin
First published in 2014 by Amie Harper

Murdoch Books Australia
83 Alexander Street
Crows Nest NSW 2065
Phone: +61 (0) 2 8425 0100
Fax: +61 (0) 2 9906 2218
murdochbooks.com.au
info@murdochbooks.com.au

Murdoch Books UK
Erico House, 6th Floor
93–99 Upper Richmond Road
Putney, London SW15 2TG
Phone: +44 (0) 20 8785 5995
murdochbooks.co.uk
info@murdochbooks.co.uk

For Corporate Orders & Custom Publishing contact
Noel Hammond, National Business Development Manager,
Murdoch Books Australia

Publisher: Jane Morrow
Editorial Manager: Virginia Birch
Design Manager: Madeleine Kane
Editor: Elle-Rose Murrell
Designer: Alice Stewart
Production Manager: Alexandra Gonzalez

A cataloguing-in-publication entry is available from the catalogue
of the National Library of Australia at nla.gov.au.

ISBN 978 1 74336 851 0 Australia
ISBN 978 1 74336 852 7 UK

A catalogue record for this book is available from the British Library.

Colour reproduction by Splitting Image Colour Studio Pty Ltd,
Clayton, Victoria
Printed by Hang Tai Printing Company Limited, China

IMPORTANT: Those who might be at risk from the effects of salmonella
poisoning (the elderly, pregnant women, young children and those
suffering from immune deficiency diseases) should consult their
doctor with any concerns about eating raw eggs.

OVEN GUIDE: You may find cooking times vary depending on the
oven you are using. For fan-forced ovens, as a general rule, set the
oven temperature to 20°C (35°F) lower than indicated in the recipe.

MEASURES GUIDE: We have used 20 ml (4 teaspoon) tablespoon
measures. If you are using a 15 ml (3 teaspoon) tablespoon add an
extra teaspoon of the ingredient for each tablespoon specified.

**All recipes are based on the author's food journey of introducing
her baby to solid foods from the age of 6 months. All props are
author's own and are for visual purposes only. Never leave your
baby alone whilst feeding and make sure all foods are finely
chopped, puréed and steamed to coincide with your babies' age
and chewing ability to prevent choking.**

REFERENCES

AUSTRALIA
World Health Organization
who.int/nutrition/topics/infantfeeding_recommendation/en
Australian Breastfeeding Association breastfeeding.asn.au
Dietitians Association of Australia daa.asn.au
**The Royal Australasian College of Physicians
(Paediatrics and Child Health Division)** racp.edu.au
The Royal Australian College of Immunology
Food & allergy information
Australasian Society of Clinical Immunology and Allergy
allergy.org.au

UK
Unicef unicef.org.uk
National Health Service nhs.uk
The Association of UK Dietitians
bda.uk.com

USA
**American Academy
of Pediatrics** aap.org
Breastfeeding USA
breastfeedingusa.org
Healthy Children
healthychildren.org